VOCAL SELECTIONS

One Touch of Venus

Lyrics by OGDEN NASH ● Music by KURT WEILL

TRO HAMPSHIRE HOUSE PUBLISHING CORP.

From the Musical Production "ONE TOUCH OF VENUS"

One Touch Of Venus

Lyrics by OGDEN NASH / Music by KURT WEILL

From the Musical Production "ONE TOUCH OF VENUS"

How Much I Love You

Lyrics by OGDEN NASH / Music by KURT WEILL

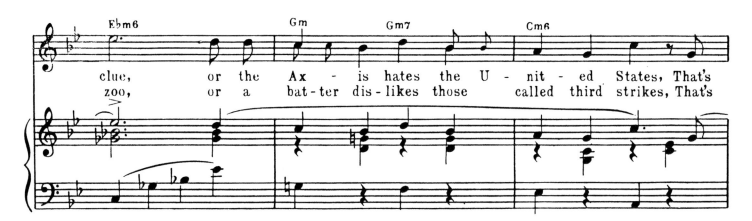

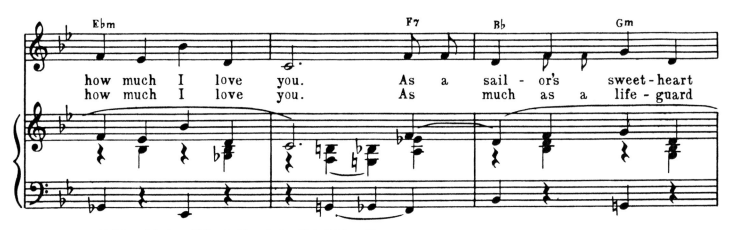

Additional lyrics: "That's How I Am Sick Of Love"

More than a mackerel hates a hook
Or a pick-pocket hates a glove
Or a Sultan hates his amorous mates
That's how I'm sick of love.
More than a hound is sick of fleas
Or "Life" is sick of "Pic"
Or a watchman yawns at beautiful dawns
That's how of love I'm sick.

I'm sick of love when the world goes right
Of love when the world goes wrong.
The silver screens and the books and magazines
They drip with love's old sweet song.
I swear to you by the earth below
And the bachelor saints above
As a secretary chokes at the boss's jokes
That's how I am sick, that's how I am sick
That's how I am sick of love.

mer-cials are a bore And more than a grape-fruit squirts. I
i - vy clad i - gloo, As a liv - er yearns for pills. I

swear to you by the stars a - bove and be - low, if such there be; As a
swear to you by the earth be - low and a - bove, if such there be; As a

bride would re - sent a bless - ed e - vent, That's how you are loved by
dachs - hund ab - hors re - volv - ing doors, That's how you are loved by

me.

me.

From the Musical Production "ONE TOUCH OF VENUS"

I'm A Stranger Here Myself

Lyrics by OGDEN NASH / *Music by* KURT WEILL

From the Musical Production "ONE TOUCH OF VENUS"

Westwind

Lyrics by OGDEN NASH / Music by KURT WEILL

Andantino, un poco agitato

I had a love and my love was fair, fair as a sum-mer's dawn. I lost my love, I nev-er knew where,

From the Musical Production "ONE TOUCH OF VENUS"

Way Out West In Jersey

Lyrics by OGDEN NASH / Music by KURT WEILL

From the Musical Production "ONE TOUCH OF VENUS"

Foolish Heart

Lyrics by OGDEN NASH / Music by KURT WEILL

Will you tell me how these things hap-pen? Have I trust-ed in love too much? When did the mag-ic van-ish? Have I some-how lost my

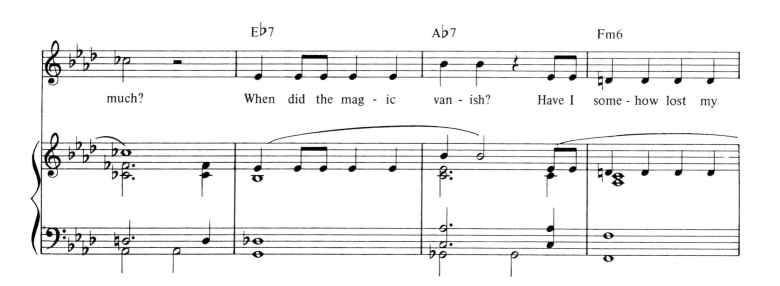

From the Musical Production "ONE TOUCH OF VENUS"

The Trouble With Women

Lyrics by OGDEN NASH / Music by KURT WEILL

24

came from a cat-bush, And she nev-er had heard of first
fered with my vis-ion, They were love-ly, vo-lup-tu-ous
lives in a trail-er, With some dev-il-may-care de-bu-
girls like a heav-y, And in-quire if they would, or would

base _____ So I trav-el no long-er to Flat-bush,
specks _____ Then I toiled on a farm till-ing soy beans,
tantes _____ Her love for her kin is ex-quis-ite,
not _____ I al-ways im-plied that they had to,

Tho' the girl is both wealth-y and pure _____ For when-
Hop-ing fresh air would cure me, per-haps _____ But the
She ___ en-ter-tains un-cles ga-lore _____ But when-
But ___ jim-min-ies, was I per-plexed _____ The

*(lyrics used in show):

"In a struggle to chasten my brain, but the girl beans got in with the boy beans, and I never struggled again."

Additional lyrics:
One weekend I rented a Packard
For a maiden of whom I was fond.
Her lips and her toenails were lacquered
And I think she was technically blond.
Her defenses had started to crumble,
I was bursting with masculine pride,
When up spoke a voice from the rumble—
Her mother had stolen a ride.

Oh, the trouble, the trouble with women,
They are constantly one jump ahead.
You touch what you think is a bosom,
And you find it's an eight-ball instead.

The reason I moan in my slumber
Is that I'm subject to female rebuffs,
Or if I make a note of a number,
The laundry erases my cuffs.
If I droop like a lily in sadness,
The diagnosis is easy to see,
Every woman has moments of madness,
But never, no never with me.

Oh, the trouble, the trouble with women,
I repeat it again and again,
From Kalamazoo to Kamchatka
The trouble with women is men.

From the Musical Production "ONE TOUCH OF VENUS"

Speak Low

Lyrics by OGDEN NASH / Music by KURT WEILL

Time is so old _____ and love so brief, Love is pure gold _____ and

time a thief. *We're late _____ dar- ling, we're late _____

The cur- tain de- scends, ev- 'ry thing ends too

soon, too soon I wait _____ dar- ling, I

wait _____ Will you speak low to me, speak love to me and soon. _____

*See next page for Duet done in original production.

Duet from stage production in original key:

Venus: It's late _____ dar - ling it's late _____ The cur - tain de - scends, ev - 'ry-thing

Rodney: It's late _____ dar - ling it's late _____ The cur - tain de - scends, ev - 'ry-thing

ends too soon _____ I wait _____ dar - ling I

ends too soon too soon I wait _____ dar - ling I

wait _____ Will you speak love to me. _____

wait _____ Will you speak low _____ to me.

Very, Very, Very

Lyrics by OGDEN NASH / Music by KURT WEILL

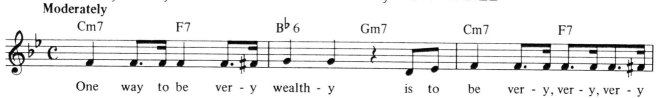

One way to be ver - y wealth - y is to be ver - y, ver - y, ver - y

rich; One can pile up mink and er - mine like a her-mit ac-cu-mu-lates ver - min, if you

oc - cu-py the prop-er fi-nan-cial niche. One way to be ver - y hap - py is to

be ver - y, ver - y, ver - y rich; There are kinds of hu - man pleas-ures that are

not to be pur-chased with treas-ures, but I can't re-mem-ber ex-act - ly which. I've

heard my gild - ed friends com - plain there are trou - bles mon-ey can-not cure. But a

trou-ble is a trou-ble is a trou-ble, and it's twice the trou-ble when a per-son is

That's Him

Lyrics by OGDEN NASH / Music by KURT WEILL

You know the way you feel when there is au-tumn in the air; That's
You know the way you feel a-bout the "Rhap-so-dy in Blue;" That's

him, That's him. The way you feel when An-toine has
him, That's him. The way you feel a-bout a hat cre-

fin-ished with your hair; That's him, That's him. You
a-ted just for you; That's him, That's him. You

From the Musical Production "ONE TOUCH OF VENUS"

Wooden Wedding

Lyrics by OGDEN NASH / Music by KURT WEILL

Moderato

Piano

I have a bliss-ful day-dream, A gay dream of you, And

dai - ly I dream of the gold-en years, When my day-dream has come true.

Refrain

Wait-ing for our wood-en wed-ding, Gol - ly, how the time will
Wait-ing for our wood-en wed-ding, Gol - ly, how the birds will

TRO VOCAL•SELECTIONS

HIGH SPIRITS — **Hugh Martin and Timothy Gray**
Forever And A Day, I Know Your Heart, If I Gave You, Something Tells Me,
Was She Prettier Than I?, You'd Better Love Me.

OLIVER! — **Lionel Bart**
As Long As He Needs Me, Be Back Soon, Boy For Sale, Consider Yourself,
Food Glorious Food, I'd Do Anything, It's A Fine Life, Oliver, Oom-Pah-Pah,
Pick A Pocket Or Two, Reviewing The Situation, Where Is Love?, Who Will Buy?

THE ROAR OF THE GREASEPAINT — **The Smell of the Crowd**
Leslie Bricusse and **Anthony Newley**
The Beautiful Land, Feeling Good, It Isn't Enough, The Joker, Look At That Face,
My First Love Song, My Way, Nothing Can Stop Me Now, Put It In The Book,
Sweet Beginning, That's What It Is To Be Young, Things To Remember, This Dream,
What A Man, Where Would You Be Without Me?, Who Can I Turn To (When Nobody
Needs Me), With All Due Respect, A Wonderful Day Like Today.

STOP THE WORLD — **I Want To Get Off** - **Leslie Bricusse** and **Anthony Newley**
All-American, Glorious Russian, Gonna Build A Mountain, I Wanna Be Rich,
Life Is A Woman, Lumbered, Meilinki Meilchik, Once In A Lifetime, Someone Nice
Like You, Typically English, Typische Deutsche, What Kind Of Fool Am I?

TAKING MY TURN — **Will Holt** and **Gary William Friedman**
Fine For The Shape I'm In, Good Luck To You, I Am Not Old, It Still Isn't Over,
Pick More Daisies, Taking My Turn, This Is My Song, Two Of Me.

U.S. $9.95

HL00378805

EXCLUSIVELY DISTRIBUTED BY
HAL•LEONARD®
CORPORATION
7777 W. BLUEMOUND RD. P.O. BOX 13819 MILWAUKEE, WI 53213

ISBN 978-0-634-02189-3